WE DO EASY

ANNABEL KUKU

70+ simple recipes - healthy, delicious, & such great fun!

WE DO EASY

_____ *70+ simple recipes - healthy, delicious, & such great fun!* _____

Contents

We Do Easy ───────────────────

Yes. That's right. We do Easy.

I love my food, mostly "pretty food". I usually opt for healthy and palatable options. A fair balance between tasty, simple and healthy is what I set out to achieve. I get there most times. Am I naughty on occasion? Of course I am!

We Do Easy was birthed by the intention of sharing ideas on meal preparation and keeping it really simple. As a commuting homemaker with a young child, it was imperative that meal preparation was quick and with minimum fuss. I aimed for thirty minutes. As a family we had a few health issues, thus having a healthy daily diet was non-negotiable. Additionally, over the years I have observed a certain vulnerability to diabetes and other chronic conditions in my community. These factors to a large extent influence my dietary preferences. If I were to rank my considerations in order of priority, it was always good nutritional value first, time efficiency came second and aesthetics third. However, they were all important to me.

I am Nigerian by origin and my formative years were spent in Nigeria; thus it is no surprise that this may be reflected in my choices, palate and culinary preferences. Oh! How I love "stew"! We had stew with everything - rice and stew, fried plantain and stew, yam and stew, and the list goes on. I cook with seasonal produce easily available from local super markets. Thus, it is no great surprise that I have been known to grace the dinner table with some unpremeditated "Afrofusion".

I have not used professional photos in this book. Grateful for the continually evolving technological advancement in mobile phones with cameras, the pictures you see here are photos of my various meals prepared in my kitchenette in Gravesend! The recipes in this book are relatable and attainable. Whenever I liked the look of a dish I prepared, I took a photo of it. It always gives me great pleasure to share with friends and family. On occasion, I derive the ultimate satisfaction of influencing their food choices e,g. a lot more fresh vegetables hidden in a burger, alternate sources of protein etc and "mach 2" the use of leftovers.

Now, I am utterly delighted to share my recipes, back stories and pictures with you.

Bon Appetit!

We Do Easy

Author: Annabel Kuku

Copyright © Annabel Kuku (2024)

The right of Annabel Kuku to be identified as author of this work has been asserted by the author in accordance with section 77 and 78 of the Copyright, Designs and Patents Act 1988.

First Published in 2024

ISBN: 978-1-83538-113-7 (Paperback)
 978-1-83538-114-4 (Hardback)
 978-1-83538-115-1 (E-Book)

Published by:
Maple Publishers
Fairbourne Drive, Atterbury,
Milton Keynes,
MK10 9RG, UK
www.maplepublishers.com

MAPLE
PUBLISHERS

A CIP catalogue record for this title is available from the British Library.

Vegetable & Pasta Mains

Butterbean Curry

1 can of butterbeans
1 can chopped tomatoes
½ tbsp tomato puree
1 large carrot - cut into
  large batons or 1 inch pieces
  (depending on your aesthetic
  preference)
100ml of water
4 broccoli florets
1 medium onion -
chopped
1 tbsp sunflower oil
1 tsp curry powder
1 large garlic clove -
  minced
1cm of ginger chopped
½ tsp chilli flakes
  (adjust according to taste)
½ tsp turmeric
½ tsp paprika
A pinch of Salt

Method

1. Heat oil in a pan on a medium heat.

2. Fry the onions for 2 minutes, then add the butter beans, garlic, ginger, chili flakes, turmeric, paprika and salt.

3. Cook for 5 minutes, add the water, and then cook for a further 5 minutes.

4. Add the tomatoes, tomato puree and curry powder.
(Alternatively, you and use tomato stew (page 38) instead of canned tomatoes).

5. Stir and leave to simmer for 3 minutes. Stir in carrots and broccoli. Cover with lid and allow to cook for 2 minutes and turn off the heat.

6. Allow to stand for a further 2 minutes (you want your vegetables crunchy, so let the steam cook them through).

Serving suggestion:
Serve with rice/ on mashed potatoes/ jacket sweet potato/ boiled maris piper or Marabel potatoes.

Asaro is a Nigerian dish otherwise known as Yam Pottage. It is made from yam (a tuber vegetable), palm oil and the tomato stew ingredients. It may include meat or fish.

One evening I fancied Asaro for dinner, but I did not have yam. I opened my refrigerator and found the below ingredients. With the fight against anaemia always in the forefront of my mind, chicken liver was the top choice for a tasty and nutritious accompaniment. Chicken liver is very rich in iron, folate, riboflavin, B6 and B12.

Asaro Fusion

Serves 1

200g Chantenay carrots
200g parsnips
200g sweet potato
200g cauliflower - sliced
Half seeded green pepper - sliced
1 small red onion - diced
4 ladles/500ml of tomato stew (page 38)
2cm fresh ginger - grated
2 cloves of garlic - diced
½ tsp dried oregano (optional)
½ tsp turmeric powder
½ tsp chilli flakes (optional)

Chicken Livers:

400g chicken livers - washed and dried with a paper towel
1 tsp garlic paste
1 tsp ginger paste
A large pinch of salt
A pinch of ground black pepper
A handful of baby spinach

Method

1. Mix garlic paste, ginger paste, salt and ground black pepper in garlic paste and ginger.

2. Rub a little sunflower oil on the dry livers then rub the seasoning into the livers cover in a dish and leave to marinate.

3. Prepare Vegetables: Give the carrots a good scrub and chop off the heads. Rinse and peel parsnip and cut into same size as carrots.. If the core of the parsnips is very fibrous you can cut away. Rinse and cut cauliflower into florets.

4. Heat tablespoon of sunflower oil in a sauce pan.

5. Add diced onions, lower heat and and stir onions for 2 minutes (I usually add the onions first to prevent the garlic from burning – you don't want that! It gives a bitter taste).

6. Add garlic and ginger, stir for a further 2 minutes and add the tomato stew and turmeric powder and bring to the boil.

7. Scoop ½ a ladle of the stew into a ramekin and crush half a chicken stock cube and return the mixture to the pot. Add the parsnips and replace lid and allow to cook for 5 minutes.

8. Add carrots and broccoli florets. Allow to cook for a further 3 mins, then add the sliced green peppers. Allow to cook for 1 minute and turn off the heat. Ensure you leave the lid on. The heat will soften the peppers but still retain the crunch.

Chicken Livers:

1. Heat a tablespoon of sunflower oil in a small frying pan. Coat livers with garlic paste, ginger paste, salt and pepper. Fry for 3 minutes on each side.

2. Check with a skewer to ensure it is cooked – a little pink on the inside but not oozing blood.

Beetroots are a great source of fibre folate (vitamin B9), manganese, nitrates, potassium, iron, and vitamin C. Beetroots have been long associated with numerous health benefits, including improved blood flow, lower blood pressure, and increased exercise performance. Carrots are a good source of beta carotene, fibre, vitamin K1, potassium, and antioxidants. Quinoa comes along with all that protein and makes it such a nutritious jamboree! This is such a 'taste-good' and 'feel good' winning combination.

Beetroot, Carrot & Quinoa Burgers ——

150g/ 2 large raw beetroot - peeled and grated
4 heaped tbsp of parboiled quinoa
100g/1 large carrot - peeled and grated
2 eggs
½ red onion - finely chopped
1 garlic clove - crushed
80g rolled oats
1 tsp salt
¼ tsp ground black pepper
¼ tsp ground chilli pepper
A handful of flat leaf parsley leaves - finely chopped
Spray oil (brand of your choice)

To Serve:
4 burger buns (Brioche for extra luxury)
2 sliced firm salad tomatoes
4 tbsp mayonnaise (reduced fat if you have your eye on the calories and fat content)
1 tbsp English mustard
A handful of shredded iceberg lettuce

Method

1. Preheat the oven to 200°C, gas mark 6.

2. In a ramekin, mix the mayonnaise and mustard; set aside.

3. In a large bowl, thoroughly combine all the ingredients for the burger, apart from the oil; set aside. Mould the beetroot mixture into 4 large burger patties, about 2cm thick, firmly compressing the mixture so it keeps its shape.

4. Spray a large non-stick pan and heat it over a medium heat. Gently put the burgers into the pan and fry for 3-4 minutes on each side until golden, then transfer to a baking tray lined with baking parchment and bake for 20 minutes. Remove and leave to cool slightly.

Serving suggestion:
Serve in the burger buns with the rocket, iceberg lettuce, tomatoes and mustard mayonnaise. For an extra kick, swap mustard mayo for a tomato chilli chutney.

Let's Pack It All In -
Black eyed beans & baked potato slices

Serves 2
Tomato stew - page 38
2 cups black eyed beans - rinsed and soaked in a bowl of room temperature water for 2 hours or overnight
3 bay leaves or 2 heaped tbsp of ground crayfish (available from most African and Afro Caribbean stores)
1 chicken stock cube
1 medium sized red onion - chopped
2 tbsp olive oil
Curly leaf parsley (for garnish)

Method

1. In a large pot pour 2 litres of water to boil. Empty the water from the soaked beans and rinse the beans.

2. When the water is boiled, add the beans and boil on high heat for 20 minutes or until soft.

3. In another pot heat the oil and fry the chopped onions for two minutes.

4. Scoop 4 large ladles of tomato stew into the frying onions. Allow it boil for two minutes and then add the bay leaves, chicken stock cube and chilli powder. Add crayfish if using. Leave to heat for 5 mins.

5. Check beans. If it is soft enough to mash, drain using a colander and add to the stew mixture. Cover and allow to cook for a further 5 – 10 minutes.

6. Turn off heat and leave to stand for 5 minutes before serving.

Serving suggestions:
Fried/grilled plantain, boiled or fried yam or garri, sautéed potatoes, mackerel

Just when you thought Kale Couldn't Party

Serves 4

2 tbsp olive oil

1 large onion - sliced

1 packet of shredded kale - washed and drained

½ Scotch bonnet - sliced (optional)

2 cloves of garlic - peeled and crushed

½ of 1 small head of broccoli - chopped

2 carrots - chopped

1 cm of ginger - scrubbed and chopped into tiny pieces

Tomato salsa – (page 91)

Falafel – (page 95)

Method

1. Heat olive oil over low heat – do not let it smoke!

2. Add onions and stir for 1 min, add garlic, ginger and scotch bonnet if using. Allow to cook for about 5 mins.

3. Put water to boil.

4. Add washed kale, carrots and broccoli. Stir thoroughly so kale is coated with the oil and spices. Moisten with a tablespoon of water. Season with a pinch of salt. Replace pot lid tightly and allow vegetables steam for 5 mins.

6. When ready, serve kale with couscous, salsa and falafel.

On one of those evenings – Rushed in from after school club, no dinner pre-prep in the morning, homework outstanding and yet a long evening ahead, so much to do and too little time. Dinner must hit the table 35 mins max! For days like this I always keep convenience foods in the cupboard.

Tuna & Pasta Bake
- We Call This Really Easy

450g wholewheat rigatoni pasta or any other tubular pasta. Penne and macaroni work well too

170g strong cheddar - grated

1 x 400g can of chicken soup - diluted with half a can of water

1.5 x 160g cans tuna steak in spring water - drained

220g sweetcorn - drained

1 large handful of chopped parsley

1 tsp ground black pepper

½ tsp garlic granules

Method

1. Heat oven to 180C/fan 160C/gas 4.

2. Boil pasta for 2 mins less time than stated on the pack.

3. Mix the water and cream of chicken soup, stir in garlic granules.

4. Drain the pasta, mix with the cream of chicken soup, drained cans of tuna, sweetcorn and a large handful of chopped parsley, then season with black pepper.

5. Transfer to a baking dish and top with the grated cheddar.

6. Bake for 15-20 mins until the cheese on top is golden and starting to brown.

7. Serve with a salad or any vegetables of your choice.

Beetroot, Butterbean & Chorizo Hash

4 cooked beetroot - cubed

1 large sweet potato - peeled and cubed

300g King Edward potatoes - peeled and cubed

½ a 400g can of butterbeans

1 whole chorizo sausage cut into 1-inch pieces

¼ tsp chilli flakes

2 tsp wholegrain mustard

2 tbsp Worcestershire sauce

4 large eggs

1 tbsp sunflower oil - plus extra for frying

Method

1. Pre-heat the oven to 190C if using a fan assisted oven set at 170C.

2. Put a pan of water to boil. When boiling, add sweet potato and King Edward potatoes.

3. Put the potatoes in a large, ovenproof dish with beetroot, butterbeans onions and chorizo. Mix together the oil, chilli powder, Worcestershire sauce and mustard, pour the mixture over the vegetables and mix well. Bake for 40 minutes, stirring halfway through.

4. Fry the eggs (sunny side up) in a little oil, place on top of the hash and serve immediately.

Asparagus Chicken Noodles

Serves 1

3 asparagus spears

1 nest of egg noodles (I used dried as I forgot to buy fresh)

1 red chilli pepper - thinly sliced

⅓ red bell pepper and ⅓ green bell pepper - cut into strips

1 fresh large chicken breast - cut into strips

100 ml chicken stock (whenever I boil chicken, I save stock in ice cube trays and jam jars for later use)

2 handfuls of spinach

2 cloves of garlic - chopped of pressed

A pinch of ground chilli powder

1 tsp grated ginger

1 tsp soy sauce

1 tsp freshly ground black pepper

2 tbsp sunflower or rapeseed oil

Method

1. Season chicken strips with salt, chilli pepper and black pepper and garlic granules.
2. Following packet instructions cook the noodles substituting water for stock. This shouldn't take longer than 4 mins. When cooked, retain about 3 tablespoons of stock and drain the rest. Place the noodles in a colander and run under cold water to stop the cooking process.
3. Heat a wok and add 1 table spoon of oil add the chicken and cook for about 7 mins (add more oil if you feel you need to).
4. Whilst the chicken is cooking scrub asparagus and place the asparagus in a steamer basket and cover. Cook on high heat. Once steam forms cook until bright green and fork-tender, 2 to 3 minutes. Remove from steamer and set aside.
5. Add the ginger, minced garlic and red onion to chicken and toss for about 1 min.
6. Add sliced peppers, spinach and noodles to the chicken in the wok and sprinkle with soy sauce. Taste for seasoning – add chilli flakes if you need to. Stir and mix for 2 mins.
7. Serve immediately on warm plates and top with asparagus.

Over time I have come to the realisation that I can have nutritious low carbohydrate meals and still treat my tastebuds to the spicy, delightful and familiar flavours that I am accustomed to. On the back of this the Caulijollof was born.

Caulijollof

Serves 2

1 tbsp olive oil

1 large head of cauliflower
- grated

½ brown onion - diced

½ green pepper - diced

½ red pepper - diced

¼ tsp smoked paprika

2 tsp tomato puree

1 large ladle of tomato stew (page 38)

Method

1. In a saucepan heat olive oil. Make sure it does not smoke. You don't want to burn the onions

2. Fry onions for a minute and add paprika and stir, add tomato puree and stir for another minute.

3. Add the stew and stir. Allow to heat through until it begins to bubble.

4. Add grated cauliflower and diced peppers and stir.

5. Lower heat, replace lid and allow to simmer for about 4 mins.

6. Turn off heat. Allow to steam for another minute before serving.

Serving suggestion:

You can serve this with some grilled chicken (my preference), or any meat or fish of your choice. I like it with a green side salad. On a summer evening I would have it with grilled seabass. Don't ask me why ��.

NB. My daughter likes sticky jollof rice so I try to replicate that with the caulifjollof. Keep an eye on the clock. If you want it nice and fluffy, do not exceed the cooking time.

I find this really tasty and indulgent, so I would spoil myself at the weekend. Never mind you can skip a few of the meats if you don't have them all. Accompanied with a glass of chilled Sancerre, it went down a treat! Bon Appetit!!

Weekend Tagliatelle

Serves 2

300g Fresh Tagliatelle (Most supermarkets sell a 300g pack)

1 handful of rocket leaves

100g sundried tomatoes 1 handful of fresh baby spinach

100g sliced Chorizo sausage

1 chicken breast - sliced into strips

8 fresh king prawns

3 tbsp olive oil

1 tsp grated ginger

2 garlic cloves - minced

2 Spring onions - sliced diagonally in 1 inch pieces

A double pinch of chilli flakes

Method

1. Following pack instructions – cook tagliatelle.

2. Heat oil in a large skillet. Do not let the oil smoke!

3. Add ginger and spring onion, allow to fry for 2 minutes.

4. Add garlic, fry for another minute and add chicken stir frying for 2 minutes.

5. Add Chorizo and chilli flakes, stir fry for another minute and then add the prawns.

6. Stir for about 2 minutes and add sun dried tomatoes.

7. Drain pasta, add to chorizo mix and toss.

8. Add spinach and rocket and toss for another minute.

9. Season with salt and black pepper if desired. Serve immediately.

Lemon Salmon Pasta

Serves 2
100g fresh tagliatelle/
spaghetti
2 skinless salmon
steaks
1 tsp sunflower oil
4 garlic cloves – minced
2 tbsp butter
A pinch of salt
½ tsp ground black
 pepper
½ tsp chilli flakes
A large pinch of dried
 thyme
3 handfuls spinach
Juice from ½ lemon

Method

1. Heat oven to 180C. Rub salmon with sunflower oil. Season with salt and pepper and bake in oven for 10 – 12 mins.

2. Cook tagliatelle/spaghetti following pack instructions.

3. In a pan over low heat – melt butter and fry garlic for 2 mins before adding chilli flakes. Turn off the heat and pour the sauce into a bowl. Add salt, lemon juice and dried thyme and set aside.

4. On a plate, flake the baked salmon.

5. Add half of the sauce back in the pan. Add flaked salmon, stir for 30 seconds and add pasta.

6. Toss pasta to ensure it is covered in sauce and salmon. Add a handful of spinach and the rest of the sauce. Stir and cook for 1 minute.

Serving suggestion:
Serve immediately with a sprinkle of freshly ground black pepper on the top.

This is an alternative to the traditional moin moin made from black eyed beans and wrapped in banana leaves. I found this lighter than black-eyed beans moin moin...(And easier to make and faster to cook)

Nugget: it has a higher protein content than black eyed beans

Lentil Moin moin & Stir-fried Kale ____

Stir fried kale (page 16 - Just when you thought.....)

2 cups red split lentils

1 inch ginger (thumb-size and peeled)

2 garlic cloves - peeled

1 large red bell pepper - chopped into chunks

1 habanero pepper

1 tsp of dried chives (optional)

1 medium onion - chopped into large chunks

80ml sunflower oil or olive oil

2 medium sized boiled eggs - cut into quarters (optional)

100g steamed tuna fillet or 1 can of tuna chunks in brine

1 cup chicken stock (either make your own – boiling seasoned chicken and bones or make from chicken stock cubes following packet instructions)

1 cup water

½ tsp salt

Method

1. Rinse the lentils in cold water and drain until water runs clear.

2. Pour the rinsed lentils into a blender/food processor, add the chopped bell pepper, onions, garlic, ginger, and habanero pepper. Add chicken stock and ½ cup of water.

3. Pour the lentil puree into a mixing bowl, add oil, dried chives and season with salt. Stir vigorously with a wooden spoon to incorporate air. It should be of pouring consistency – like a slightly grainy smoothie. Add a little water if it is thick or heavy.

4. Break up tuna chunks with a fork and stir into the mixture.

5. In a large cooking pot, bring water to boil (about 1 inch deep). Pour mixture into ramekins or other heatproof jars. If using eggs push 1 piece all the way to the bottom of each jar and place one on the top.

6. Place jars in boiling water and allow to steam for 20 minutes.

7. Check with a table knife – if cooked it should feel like a deep omelette or a quiche. Turn off the heat and leave to stand for 5 minutes before serving.

Serving suggestion:

Serve as an accompaniment with garri (ground cassava), custard, corn pap, dodo (fried/grilled plantain), jollof rice, fried rice etc. It is just as delicious on its own.

See inside of the back cover for picture of lentil moin moin in ramekins.

Brown Lentil & Vegetable Curry
on a Bed of Courgetti

Serves 1

200g brown lentils
2 tbsp rapeseed oil/sunflower oil
1x 300g can black beans
200g sweet corn (I tend to use frozen most times)
1x 400g can peeled cherry tomatoes
1 onion - chopped
1 tsp ground cumin
1 tbsp Madras curry powder
½ tsp chilli flakes
1l vegetable stock
200g green beans - trimmed and cut into short lengths
½ small bunch coriander or parsley - chopped

Method

1. Heat the oil in a large pan and fry the onion for a few mins until softened. Add the spices and cook for 1 min, then stir in the lentils, stock and the cherry tomatoes.

2. Bring to the boil, then cover and simmer for 20 mins until the lentils are tender. Add the green beans, sweetcorn and black beans. Cook for 3 mins.

3. Sprinkle the coriander or parsley and serve over courgetti. Rice and/or naan bread are good accompaniments too.

Mangetout – 100gm is only 38kcal, 3.6gm protein, 4.1gm carb and 54gm Vit C! It is filling too.

Spicy Mangetout Party —————————

Serves 2 with accompaniment or 1 if served on its own

Method

1 chicken breast fillet
2 tsp light soy sauce
¼ tsp freshly ground
 black pepper
¼ tsp chilli flakes
1 handful of washed and
 trimmed curly kale
2 tsp cornflour (optional –
 for some reason I didn't fancy
it that evening)
1 red, yellow or orange
 pepper - sliced
2 tbsp sunflower/olive oil
100g mangetout - trimmed
1 tbsp any hot and spicy
 stir fry sauce
(Alternatively – 1 crushed
garlic, ¼ finely chopped
onion and a pinch of chilli
flakes)
100ml water

1. Cut chicken fillet in three pieces and place in a bowl. Marinate with light soy sauce, hot and spicy fry sauce or alternate seasoning and cornflour. Ensure chicken is thoroughly coated in the mixture and set aside for 15 minutes.

2. Heat wok or large frying pan. Add 1 tbsp of oil. When the oil is hot add the chicken and stir-fry for 3 minutes.

3. Transfer the chicken to a plate with a slotted spoon.

4. Wipe the pan and heat it. Add the remaining oil. When it is hot, stir-fry the curly kale for 3 minutes. Add the mangetout and the pepper strips to the wok and stir-fry for another minute.

5. Lastly, add the chicken to the wok or frying pan, along with the sauce and water. If using cornflour, mix with approx. 30mls of water and stir into the wok. Mix properly.   Taste for seasoning. Adjust to your preference.

Serving suggestion:
Serve with rice, fine egg noodles or on its own

Doing it Easy on the Low Carb

Spicy Air Fryer Crispy Chicken Wings and Courgetti Medley

6 chicken wings
2 tbsp olive oil
1 tbsp grated ginger
2 cloves of garlic - chopped
2 tbsp soy sauce
360g spring greens - rinsed and sliced
3 large flat white mushrooms
3 asparagus spears
1 courgette - spiralised or thinly sliced
1 chilli pepper - cored and sliced in strips

Chicken seasoning:
1 tbsp smoked paprika
1 tbsp chilli powder
1½ tsp ground cumin 1½ tsp onion powder
1½ tsp ground black pepper
1 tsp salt

Method

Spicy Air Fryer Crispy Chicken Wings

1. Rinse chicken wings and pat dry with kitchen towel and place in a large bowl. Drizzle with oil and toss to thoroughly coat.

2. In a small bowl add smoked paprika, chilli powder, ground cumin, onion powder, garlic powder, salt and ground black pepper. Sprinkle over chicken and toss until evenly covered. Store any leftover seasoning in an empty jar to use next time.

3. Set air fryer to 190°C.

4. Arrange chicken in air fryer basket, ensuring you do not place pieces on top of each other.

5. Cook for about 6 mins, turn over and cook for another 6 mins or until juices run clear.

6. For extra crispiness, increase temperature to 200°C and leave for a further 4 mins.

Courgetti Medley

1. Heat the oil in the wok – add the garlic, ginger and chilli and fry for about 1 min.

2. Add the courgette and fry for 1 min and remove the courgette with a slotted spoon. The courgette would have released its juices.

3. Add soy sauce, asparagus and mushrooms and spring greens. Stir fry vegetables, tasting for flavour –adjust to preference. Stir fry for 3 minutes. Add in courgetti, stir through and serve immediately.

This is a hearty rich tomato sauce that can be served with anything. You can pour it over boiled rice, you can serve it with boiled or fried plantain (dodo), yam boiled or fried. It works over boiled black eyed beans. It is a delicious dip for sweet potato fries. Pour it over pasta. You can even dip your bread! As a teenager I only ate white bread and it was the best combination ever!

Nigerian Tomato Stew _____

Serves 12

12 sweet plum tomatoes
(chopped) or 3 cans of whole plum tomatoes
4 red bell peppers - chopped
2 large red onions
2 bay leaves
½ tube of tomato puree or 720g
2 large scotch bonnet peppers
4 long sweet peppers
6 cloves garlic
1 tsp of salt
120 ml chicken or beef stock
200ml sunflower oil/olive oil
1½ tsp paprika
2 tsp curry powder

Method

1. In a blender place tomatoes, onions, tomato puree, sweet peppers red onions, scotch bonnet peppers, salt, garlic cloves and water. If you have a regular blender like mine you might need to split your ingredients in two and blend one lot first. Puree until smooth.

2. Heat oil in a large pot over medium to high heat.

3. Add the blended tomato mix to the hot oil, and allow to cook for 10 minutes, stirring a few times.

4. Add curry powder, paprika and tomato puree and stir. After 5 mins add stock.

5. Allow to boil over medium heat for a further 10 minutes or until the stew has thickened.

6. Turn off the heat. Remove the bay leaves from the stew. Leaving them in may result in a bitter taste.

7. Allow stew sit for 10 minutes before serving.

I store my stew in a number of jars labelled and dated and stored in the freezer. It can keep for up to six months, but I store mine for three months at the maximum. Adding different herbs and spices depending on the dish, I would use this as a sauce for Bolognese, Chilli Con Carne, Chicken Stew, Beef Stew, Butter Bean Curry etc. E.g. for Jollof Rice I would add bay leaves to the stew, for Bolognese I would add some mixed herbs.

This is just a variation to the basic Tomato Stew recipe above.

Nigerian Chicken Stew ———————

Serves 12

6 - 12 pieces of chicken thighs or drumsticks or a combination both (vary number of pieces depending on the quantity of your stew. You can substitute chicken with beef or goat meat)

1 tsp ground black pepper

1 tsp salt

1 tsp thyme

40 ml Sunflower oil

Method

1. Rub spices on the chicken and place in a bowl and cover for twenty minutes.

2. Heat oil in a large frying pan or skillet over medium heat. (I test for readiness with a pinch of salt. It should dissolve immediately upon contact).

3. Add the chicken pieces one at a time and brown on the side for about eight minutes. Turn them over and brown on the other side.

4. Take them out and place on a piece of kitchen towel to absorb oil.

5. Add chicken to stew at Step 5 in the Nigerian Tomato recipe above.

You can follow the method above for Beef Stew and Goat Meat Stew.

Soups & Salads

Super Salad

Serves 1

½ **avocado**

2 **large pickled beetroots**
 - 1 sliced and 1 quartered

4 **baby plum tomatoes** -
 rinsed

¼ **cucumber** - sliced
 length ways

1 **hard boiled egg**

Balsamic Vinaigrette:
3 **parts of olive oil**
1 **part of balsamic vinegar**
1 **pinch of pepper**
 (optional)
1 **clove crushed garlic**
 (optional)
For a little more sweetness
 - add a little honey

Method

1. In an empty jar, add 60 ml of olive oil, 20 ml of balsamic vinegar.

2. Add pinch of pepper and/or a pinch of crushed garlic if using.

3. Replace lid firmly and shake vigorously to combine. Set aside for flavours to develop.

4. Arrange your prepared vegetables in a dish – This is my preferred arrangement. I like pretty food sometimes.

Tip:
To prevent the other half of the avocado from turning brown – place in a bowl of water, flesh side down and replace lid and store in the fridge. It should keep for up to four days.

Broccoli Salad

Serves 1

Half small red cabbage – finely sliced or shredded
4 large carrots – grated
1 head broccoli – chopped into small pieces
100g dried cranberries
100g unsalted cashew nuts - roasted

For the dressing:
1 medium red onion - chopped
90g brown sugar 60ml apple cider vinegar
2 tbsp Dijon mustard
2 tsp celery salt
¼ tsp black pepper
¼ tsp poppy seed
120ml olive oil

Method

1. Combine vegetables in a bowl, set aside the cashew nuts and cranberries for serving.

2. Place onion, dijon mustard, apple cider vinegar, brown sugar, celery salt, black pepper and poppy seed in a food processor and blend until smooth.

3. Whilst the machine is still running, slowly pour the olive oil down the feed tube in a steady stream until the dressing is emulsified. This should take about 30 seconds.

4. Sprinkle cashew nuts and cranberries over salad just before serving.

What you see is what you get....

Avocado Salad _____

Serves 1

3 iceberg leaves - torn

1 boiled egg - quartered

A handful of cherry tomatoes

¼ cucumber - rinsed and cubed

1 ripe avocado - quartered
If you feel it is a little dry - a few drops of virgin oil will cheer it up a bit.

If you want to crank it up a notch - Spicy Avocado Salad:

2 medium avocados

¾ large cucumber

3 tbsp fresh lime juice (lemon as an alternative)

A handful of chopped curly-leaf parsley

2 tbsp extra-virgin olive oil

1 jalapeno - seeds and membrane removed

½ tsp small garlic clove

¼ tsp Himalayan salt (fine sea salt as an alternative)

1 tsp Tabasco pepper sauce

Method

1. In the bottom of a salad bowl, whisk the lime juice, olive oil, garlic, jalapeno, and salt together. Stir in the herbs. You can make this dressing in advance and store in the refrigerator. I tend to make mine the night before. This allows the flavours to blend.

2. Rinse cucumber and cut four ways and cube.

3. When ready to serve the salad, rinse and dry avocados. Cut the avocados in half, remove the pits, cut into cubes and peel off the skin.

4. Add the cucumber and avocado to the bowl with the dressing. Gently toss the avocado and cucumber around the bowl so that they are well coated in the dressing.

5. Still want an extra kick? Add a few drops of Tabasco sauce

Serving Suggestion:
Scrumptious on its own. Makes a tasty full lunch when paired with pan fried salmon or seabass and tender mashed potatoes.

In Nigeria we made a salad that had everything in it. No party menu or special occasion was complete without it!

Salad of my Youth

Serves 1

¼ white cabbage - washed and thinly sliced

3 carrots, washed - peeled and grated

4 large tomatoes - washed, deseeded and chopped

¾ large cucumber - washed and chopped

A handful of little gem lettuce - washed and shredded to bits

3 large eggs - boiled and sliced

1 large Maris Piper potato (Back in the day, we just bought any potatoes available at the greengrocers)

Method

1. Wrap an oval tray with cling film.

2. Taking a handful of sliced cabbage spread on the tray, after that spread a layer of carrots, continue to add the vegetables in layers. Eggs on the top. Drizzle some salad cream over it and start to layer again until you have exhausted your piles of vegetables and drizzle some salad cream over the top.

Serving suggestion:
Serve on its own or as a side with jollof rice, fried rice, moin moin, grilled chicken or grilled fish.

Brown Lentil Soup

Serves 4

150g brown lentils
6 carrots - finely chopped
3 garlic cloves - minced
2 medium sized leeks - sliced
1.75l vegetable stock
½ tsp chilli powder (optional)
A small handful of chopped parsley - to serve

Method

1. Heat the stock in a large pot and add the lentils. Bring to a boil and allow the lentils to soften for a few minutes.

2. Add the vegetables and garlic. Season with chilli powder (if using) and salt. I often tend to skip the salt as I find store bought vegetable stock cubes sufficiently salty.

3. Bring to a boil, then reduce the heat, cover and simmer for 45-60 mins or until the lentils have broken down. Alternatively, allow to simmer for 30 mins and give a quick whizz with a hand blender if you prefer a smoother consistency. *(I tend to do the latter. On a cold day it feels like an effortless warm hug��)*

4. Scatter chopped parsley over each serving.

Serving suggestion:
It is fine on its own. It is one of those I call an 'independent' soup. On a night of indulgence, it was Agege bread. A buttered baguette or roll works too.

Chilli Carrot Soup

Serves 4 - 6

6 medium-sized carrots - peeled and chopped
2 tbsp unsalted butter
1 large white onion - chopped
4 garlic cloves - chopped
1 tsp dried thyme
950ml vegetable stock
½ tsp salt
1 tsp curry powder

Garnish:
½ tsp chilli flakes
A pinch of fresh parsley
1 tsp unflower seeds (optional)

This keeps in the fridge for about 4 -5 days and freezes for up to 6 months. On a winter's morning I would bring out a zip lock bag of soup from the freezer and I know dinner's ready in 10 minutes when I get back from work.

Method

1. In a large pot over medium heat, add the butter and onions. Cook for 3 minutes or until the onions turn translucent. Don't let them burn (it leaves a bitter taste). Season with a pinch of salt, curry powder and chilli powder.

2. Add the carrots, garlic, and dried thyme and stir. Cook for about 30 seconds, just until garlic becomes fragrant.

3. Add the vegetable stock and bring mixture to a simmer. Cover and simmer for 15 more minutes until the carrots are very tender.

4. When the carrots are tender, use a hand blender right in the pot to blend soup until smooth.

5. If you don't have a hand blender, turn off the heat on the soup and allow it to cool until it loses a lot of the steam. Depending on the size of your blender, you can blend in about two batches, and return it to the pot. Put on low heat for a few minutes.

6. Garnish with chilli flakes, sunflower seeds and fresh parsley and serve.

Oxtail & Carrot Pepper Soup

Serves 1

1.5kg oxtail - cut into small pieces (the butchers do a good job of this)

1 medium onion - chopped

2 habanero peppers - chopped **or**

1 tsp chilli flakes

3 tbsp ground crayfish

1 handful of chopped African basil (also known as Efirin and available in most African grocery stores, Etsy, Amazon and Ebay) **or 1 sprig of fresh basil** - chopped

1 tbsp Pepper Soup spice (available in most African grocery stores, Etsy, Amazon & Ebay)

1 beef bouillon cube or powder (optional)

500g Chantenay carrots - scrubbed

750ml water

Method

1. In a large pot, bring water to the boil.. Add meat and season with salt.

2. Allow to boil for 3 minutes and add ground crayfish.

3. Add pepper soup spice and chopped habanero peppers. Taste for salt. Adjust seasoning to your taste.

4. Leave to cook until oxtail is tender. Reduce heat and add the scrubbed carrots and allow to simmer for 3 mins. Add basil, and allow to simmer for a minute and turn off heat. Leave to stand for 5 mins and then serve.

Serving suggestion:
NB. For a filling meal, why not add some washed and chopped yam or potatoes when oxtail is half-cooked and leave to cook.
This keeps in the fridge for up to 5 days.

Catfish & yam Pepper Soup

Serves 1

500g fresh catfish (about 3 pieces)

150g yam (¼ of a medium sized tuber of yam) - peeled and cut into cubes

1 tbsp ground crayfish

1 tbsp pepper soup spice mix

1 medium red onion - chopped

1 tsp chilli powder or chilli flakes or ½ medium scotch bonnet pepper - chopped

1 Bouillon cube

1 tbsp African Basil leaves also known as 'Efirin' or 'scent leaf' ('Efirin' can be purchased from most African- Caribbean shops)

Salt to taste

Method

1. In a pot, put 500ml of water to boil. Ensure it is sufficient to cover the yam. When the water starts to boil, add salt to taste and the pieces of yam. Leave to boil for about 10 minutes.

2. Wash fish with hot water to remove any slime. Place in another pot, add chopped onions, seasoning cube and salt to taste. Leave to boil for about 5 minutes.

3. Add the precooked yams, pepper soup spice, pepper, ground crayfish, and the chopped basil leaves/Efirin. Leave to simmer for 5 mins.

4. Turn off heat and leave to stand for 5 mins before serving.

Meat Dishes

Lemon Chicken Wings ———————

Serves 1

3 garlic cloves - minced

Marinade:

2½ tbsp lemon juice

1 tsp lemon zest

2 tbsp olive oil

1 tbsp honey

¼ tsp paprika

¼ tsp chilli flakes

1 pinch of salt

3 dashes ground black pepper

1 tbsp chopped Parsley leaves

Method

1. Mix all the ingredients for the marinade in a bowl, whisk to combine well. Marinate the chicken in a bowl or in a plastic bag for 30 minutes, or best for 2 hours. (Chances are that after a day at work I may not have the luxury of time in the evening. I marinate it in the morning and leave in the refrigerator).

2. Pre heat the oven at 200C. Place chicken on a tray lined with parchment paper, put in the oven for about 15-20 minutes.

Alternatively, pan-fry on a skillet on medium to low heat. If you like pretty food, serve with some lemon wedges. I forgot to save some lemon!

Serving suggestion:

I served it with Waldorf Salad and a green salad – see page 61.

Whilst visiting my father-in-law for the first time whilst he was on holiday in England, he served us some roast chicken, a Waldorf Salad, potato salad and a green garden salad, all accompanied with chilled Sauvignon Blanc. I was a tad sceptical about nuts in my salad. One forkful and it was love at first bite! (Cheesy? I know). I had a second helping. When I asked if he had prepared and laid out the spread, with a cheeky laugh he replied "All professionally and lovingly laid out by my chef Waitrose!" May he rest in perfect peace. A Waldorf Salad has been a favourite ever since.

Waldorf Salad

Serves 1

6 tbsp mayonnaise (or plain yogurt)
1 tbsp lemon juice
½ tsp kosher salt
A double pinch of freshly ground black pepper
2 sweet apples - cored and chopped
1 cup seedless red grapes - halved, or ¼ cup sultanas
1 cup thinly sliced celery 1 cup chopped - slightly toasted walnuts
A few lettuce leaves

Method

Make the dressing:

1. In a medium sized bowl, whisk together the mayonnaise (or yogurt), lemon juice, salt and pepper.

2. Shred the lettuce to bits. If serving as a side dish save a few lettuce leaves for serving.

3. Stir the apple, celery, grapes/sultanas, shredded lettuce and walnuts into the bowl with the dressing.

4. Serve immediately with some chicken or spoon salad onto a bed of fresh lettuce and serve.

Green Salad:

If you want to have a green salad as well, don't overthink it. Some rocket, some spinach and throw in a handful of cherry tomatoes (yes, I know they are not green ��), you'll be just fine.

Chicken Cashew

Serves 1

For the chicken:
A double pinch sea salt
500g skinless chicken
breast fillets -sliced
1 tsp freshly ground black
 pepper
300ml groundnut oil

For the stir fry:
1 onion - sliced
A handful of mangetout
A handful of chopped
 broccoli (optional)
A handful of kale
3 tbsp chicken stock
2-3 tbsp light soy sauce
2 large spring onions -
 sliced
4 tbsp roasted cashew
nuts
A pinch sea salt (optional)
¼ ground white pepper
Steamed jasmine rice - to
serve

Serving Suggestion: I had mine
with some leftover fried rice.

Method

1. Heat a wok until smoking and add the groundnut oil. Fry the chicken for 4-5 minutes, then remove with a slotted spoon and drain on absorbent kitchen towel.

2. Scrape any left over oil into a saucer. Heat wok and toast cashew nuts in the wok for 2 mins until brown. Remove from heat and save cashews on a plate.

3. Stir fry: Reheat the oil over high heat (add a little oil if you have to). Add the kale, broccoli and mangetout.

4. Add the chicken pieces and stir fry for 1-2 minutes, then add the stock and soy sauce. Simmer for another minute, or until the chicken is cooked through.

3. Stir in the spring onions and cashew nuts, season with sea salt (if using) and ground white pepper and transfer to a serving dish. Serve immediately.

Chicken
Chilli Rose

Serves 1

1 large onion - diced
1 red pepper or carrot - diced
2 large garlic cloves -
 chopped
1 tbsp oil
1 heaped tsp hot chilli powder (we like chilli)
1 tsp paprika
1 tsp ground cumin
500g minced chicken
300ml chicken stock -
 (made from chicken stock
 cube or made from boiling
 chicken)
1x 400g can chopped
 tomatoes
1 tsp sugar (optional)
2 tbsp tomato purée
410g can red kidney beans
1 brown tortilla to serve
Sour cream to serve
 (optional)

Shortcut
Follow steps 1 – 3, add 400ml of tomato stew (equivalent of one can of tomato sauce) and carry on from step 7.

After a long day, I find the shortcut most appealing!

Method

1. In a saucepan heat up oil over a medium heat. Add the onion, stirring and allow to cook for about 5 minutes or until onion is translucent.

2. Add the garlic, red pepper/carrot, hot chilli powder, paprika and cumin ground cumin. Stir and leave it to cook for another 3 minutes, stirring occasionally.

3. When it begins to sizzle add the chicken mince and break up with a wooden spoon.

4. Keep stirring for about 4 minutes. Add chicken stock and chopped tomatoes. Tip in the sugar if using. Add a good shake of salt and pepper. Add tomato puree and stir.

5. Replace lid and allow to simmer for about 15 minutes.

6. Stir sauce intermittently to prevent it from drying out or sticking to the pan. If it is drying out, add a couple of tablespoons of water and turn down the heat. After simmering gently, the saucy mince mixture should look thick, moist and juicy.

7. Heat oven at 200C.

8. Stir kidney beans into the sauce. Bring to the boil again for another 5 minutes, taste for seasoning. Adjust to your preference.

9. Turn off the heat and leave to stand for 10 minutes before serving. This is really important as it allows the flavours to mingle.

10. Fold foil in a shape to support tortilla. Fit tortilla in foil shape to form flower and heat in the oven for 5 minutes.

11. Scoop chilli into tortilla flower and top with a dollop of sour cream if desired. Break off crispy tortilla, scoop chilli and enjoy!

I made this for the first time for a barbeque.

Shout out to my daughter. She plated this...On its second outing we had it with rice.

Loved Up Pork Belly _____

Serves 2 as a meal

4 pork belly slices

1 tsp curry powder

1 tsp chilli powder

1 tsp garlic powder (garlic granules work too)

2 tbsp sunflower oil

1 cucumber - peeled, deseeded and cut into strips (do not discard seeds)

½ tsp salt

Just in case you're wondering "What happened to the cucumber?" If having it with rice, here we go:

1 tbsp sunflower/olive oil

1 clove of garlic - chopped

½ inch piece of ginger - finely chopped

½ bunch spring onions - rinsed and chopped

1 tsp chilli flakes (or less depending on your taste)

1 tsp sugar (I use unrefined cane sugar)

2 tsp sesame oil

125ml water

A pinch of salt

Method

1. In a saucer, combine spices and salt.

2. Dry pork belly slices with a paper towel and rub sunflower oil over pork belly slices. Then rub the spice mix all the pork belly slices, taking time to rub the spices into the meat. Place on a plat and cover with clingfilm for 30 minutes minimum. Alternatively, leave overnight in the refrigerator.

3. Heat a BBQ and place the meat on it for 15 mins.

4. Turn it over and grill for a further 15 mins. If using the oven place in a preheated oven 200 degrees/180 (fan assisted) for 17 mins turn over and cook for a further 15 mins.

5. When cooked Allow to stand for 5 minutes and cut into bite sized pieces.

Make Garnish: Peel a cucumber and roll some strips of the peel. Hold together with a cocktail stick. With the rest, make a lattice on a plate.

If serving with rice:

1. Place the cucumber in a bowl and sprinkle with ½ tbsp salt. Mix thoroughly and tip into a colander and leave to drain for 20 mins. This helps rid the cucumbers of excess water. Rinse the cucumbers thoroughly to rid them of the salt and pat dry with kitchen towel.

2. Blend cucumber seeds in 125ml of water and set aside (This is optional. Nothing edible goes to waste in my kitchen. If you choose to skip this, set the water aside).

3. Heat a wok over high heat and add oil. When the oil is hot, add ginger, spring onion and garlic and stir-fry for 30 seconds.

4. Add the cucumbers, chilli flakes, sugar, , and cook for a further 30 seconds. Tossing until everything is well mixed. Add 125ml water / blended cucumber seed mix and continue to stir-fry over high heat for 3 mins until the cucumbers are cooked and most of the water has evaporated. Stir in the sesame oil to serve.

Happy! Fresh or 'Mach 2'

Beef

Serves 1

Sauce:

2 tbsp cornstarch / cornflour

62 ml water

1 tbsp dark soy sauce

1½ tbsp light soy sauce

1 tbsp Chinese cooking wine or mirin. Dry sherry works almost as good

¼ tsp Chinese five spice powder

1 tsp sesame seed oil (optional)

¼ tsp black pepper

Stir fry:

2 tbsp oil

360g beef fillet, flank or rump – if using fresh. I used some left over boiled beef I had in the fridge

2 garlic cloves - finely chopped

1 tsp fresh ginger - finely chopped

1 head of broccoli - split the florets

A handful of spring green leaves

2 carrots - chopped

1 cup water

Method

1. Place cornflour and water in bowl then mix. Add remaining sauce ingredients (water, dark soy sauce, light soy sauce, sesame oil, Chinese five spice and wine). Stir vigorously.

2. Slice the beef into 1/4" / 0.5cm thick slices.

3. Place the beef and 2 tbsp of the sauce into a bowl and set aside.

4. Heat oil in a skillet over high heat. Add beef and spread out, leave for 1 minute until browned.

5. Stir fry beef for 10 seconds, then add garlic and ginger. Stir for another 30 seconds or until beef is no longer pink (if using fresh).

6. Pour sauce and water into the skillet and quickly mix.

7. When the sauce starts bubbling, add the vegetables. Stir to coat the broccoli in sauce, then let it simmer for 2 minute or until sauce is thickened.

8. Remove from heat immediately and serve over rice. Sprinkle with sesame seeds if desired.

Sticky Rack'O'Ribs & Steamed Vegetables

Serves 1

1kg rack of pork ribs –
(you can also buy individual ribs)
2 garlic cloves - crushed 500g carton passata
2 tbsp soy sauce
3 tbsp honey
1 tbsp Worcestershire auce

Method

1. Heat oven to 200°C/fan 180°C/Gas Mark 6.

2. In a large bowl, mix the garlic, soy sauce, honey, passata and Worcestershire sauce.

3. Place the pork ribs in the bowl and mix well to coat evenly. Place ribs in a large, shallow roasting tin and cover with sauce. Cover with foil and bake for 35 mins.

4. Remove foil from tray and bake the ribs for a further 45 mins, turning them a couple of times, until sticky and almost all of the sauce has disappeared.

Tip:
I usually half-cook the ribs the night before and leave in the refrigerator overnight until I need them.

Serving suggestion:
Serve with vegetable fried rice, fried yam chips or potato fries. I didn't fancy any of that - I was just happy with some steamed vegetables.

Brown Rice & Black Eyed Beans
with Goat Meat Stew

Serves 1

1 cup of brown Basmati rice

½ cup of black eyed beans

Goat Meat Stew (page 40)

3 cups of water (for boiling)

Method

1. Soak black eyed beans in water overnight (or for 2 hours).

2. Put 3 cups of water to boil in a large pot. Rinse the beans and add to the boiling water and leave to boil for 20 mins.

3. Rinse rice and add to the boiling beans. Season with salt.   Boil rice until soft.

Serving suggestion:

Serve with goat meat stew and steamed vegetables.

Chicken Livers - Peri-Peri Style

Serves 1

400g chicken livers
3 cloves of garlic - crushed
Freshly ground dry chilli
pepper - for quantity be
 guided by your taste buds
Double pinch salt
1½ tbsp of butter
3 tbsp Peri-peri sauce
3 cloves of garlic
125ml cup whipped
cream (full fat or half fat)
(optional)
 Juice of 1 lemon
1 handful of chopped
 parsley

Method

1. Rinse livers and pat dry with a kitchen towel. Slice livers into manageable pieces and trim any fat.

2. Heat a large pan or skillet over high heat. The pan must be very hot in order to sear the livers and cook them quickly.

3. Add the butter to the skillet and add the livers. Allow to brown well on both sides

4. Once they are golden brown on both sides, add the Peri-peri sauce and garlic. Allow to fry for about 3 mins and garlic releases its aroma and the Peri-peri sauce starts to dry out.

5. Add the cream and lemon juice. Season to taste with salt and pepper and allow to simmer for another 5 minutes.

Serving suggestion:
It was an 'empty the fridge' day, so it was grilled plantain, jollof rice and cabbage. When I go heavy with the cream, I serve with a baguette.

As I grow older I am not oblivious to the deceleration of my metabolism. Growing up in Nigeria, we were raised on carbs – rice, yam, cassava etc. Many years ago I could eat a carb dense three course meal for lunch and by dinner time I'd be ready to do it all over again. I find that I cannot handle it now. Thus, I try to eat less carbohydrate than I used to, but ensure I enjoy it too.

grilled Chicken & Stir Fried Vegetables

Marinade for Chicken:
1 tsp black pepper
1 tsp salt
1 tsp garlic granules
1tsp smoked paprika
1 tbsp sunflower oil

Method

1. Add all ingredients to a bowl and mix well.

2. If you like chicken skin, keep it on, if you don't, peel it off (or buy skinless). Massage the marinade into the chicken. Lift the skin and rub marinade on the chicken flesh.

3. Leave to marinate for half an hour at room temperature. (When I wake up with my thinking cap on I tend to do it in the morning and place in a freezer bag and leave it in the refrigerator)

4. Heat oven at 200°C.

5. After marinating, set chicken on a baking tray lined with parchment paper and place in the middle of the oven. I line with parchment paper because I don't have to grease it and it doesn't stick!

6. Turn the chicken over after 20 minutes. Leave for another 20 minutes.

7. Pierce with a metal skewer or knife to check that juices run clear. If cooked through and tender, bring out of the oven and allow to stand.

Grilled Chicken & Stir Fried Vegetables
contd..

I would start on the stir-fried vegetables when there is about 10 minutes to go on the chicken.

Stir Fried vegetables:

4 broccoli florets - sliced vertically

4 cauliflower florets - sliced vertically

2 spring onions - sliced diagonally

A handful of carrot batons

¼ scotch bonnet pepper - diced

1 tsp soy sauce

½ tbsp olive oil

Method

1. Heat the sunflower oil in a wok for ½ a minute.

2. Lower heat and vegetables, sprinkle garlic granules over vegetables and a splash or two of soy sauce depending on your preference. Stir fry for 3 minutes

3. Add spring onions. Stir fry for 1 min and serve immediately with oven baked chicken.

As a working mum with a young child, there were some evenings when all I wanted to do was get her fed! This recipe worked. Mixed beans do not come with the additional salt and sugar found in baked beans'

TriBean & Sausage Casserole _____

Serves 4

1 red onion - chopped
2 tbsp of olive oil
2 cans of mixed beans - drained and rinsed
1 ramekin of sweetcorn
1 can of chopped tomato with herbs (If pressed for time whip out some tomato stew from the freezer and heat in the microwave for 3 minutes)
½ tsp chilli flakes
½ tsp of curry powder
1 chicken stock cube
4 baking potatoes – Maris Piper and King Edward are fluffy when baked
2 Cumberland sausages,
2 plain pork sausages/ chicken sausages
1 chorizo sausage

Serving suggestion:
Serve the bean and sausage casserole in split jacket potatoes with a side salad.

Boiled or fried potatoes are a good substitute for baked. Baked sweet potato works a treat too.

Method

1. Scrub potatoes and poke them with a fork (this helps the heat escape during the heating process and prevents a potato explosion in your microwave oven) and place potatoes in the microwave and cook for 6 minutes.

2. Chop up the chorizo sausage and set aside. Following pack instructions – poke the other sausages and place on the grill.

3. Heat a medium sized saucepan and add the oil and chopped onions and chorizo. Fry on low heat for 2 mins.

4. If using canned chopped tomatoes - add this to the onion and chorizo mix and stir in the chilli flakes, allow to cook for 5 mins (If using tomato stew, it doesn't need to cook for 5 mins). Then add the curry powder and chicken stock cube allow to cook for another 4 minutes.

5. Chop up the grilled sausages and add to the tomato mix.

6. Add drained beans and sweetcorn and stir. Cover with lid. Turn down the heat and allow to heat through for 4 mins and then take it off the hob.

7. Split the baked sweet potato down the middle and scoop out the flesh with a tablespoon or ice cream scoop.

Oh! I had fantasized about this dish all day. Only to realise it was a low carb week, so no rice and I didn't have caulirice either. It was a small serving on its own and an early night to avoid temptation!

Sweet & Savoury Peppers & Chicken —

Serves 1

225g (about 2 medium) chicken breast - cut into 1-inch pieces
2 tbsp olive oil
1 yellow/red bell pepper - cut into 1-inch squares of your preferred shape
1 tsp chilli flakes
1 tsp grated ginger
1 tbsp Sriracha sauce or your favourite hot sauce
2 tsp freshly ground black pepper
1 green bell pepper - cut into 1-inch squares of your preferred shape
3 tbsp cornflour
3 garlic cloves - minced
1 tbsp brown sugar or honey
40ml low sodium soy sauce
2 tsp sesame oil

Method

1. Rub black pepper into chicken breast and set aside.

2. Stir fry sauce: In a small bowl, whisk the Sriracha, garlic, sesame oil, ginger, soy sauce, brown sugar and cornflour. This is your stir-fry sauce.

3. Heat one tablespoon of olive oil in a skillet over medium heat. Fry the diced bell peppers for 2 mins, but still al dente.

Remove the peppers from the skillet and set aside on a plate.

4. Add 1 tbsp of oil to the skillet and turn up the heat. Add the chicken. Turn over to ensure chicken is seared on both sides. Reduce heat to medium and continue to cook for 2 mins. Pierce with a fork to ensure it is no longer pink.

5. Add the peppers back to the skillet and pour the stir-fry sauce over the chicken and peppers. Simmer for 1-2 minutes until the sauce starts to thicken. Add a little water if the sauce gets too thick. Turn off heat and serve immediately.

Accompaniment: Rice, cauliflower rice, courgetti
Tip: Why not crank it up a notch? Sprinkle some toasted sesame seeds over it just before serving.

Sandwiches, Wraps & More

Easy Like Saturday Morning

Serves 1

1 or 2 eggs – what do you fancy?

½ - 1 wholemeal tortilla wrap (folded in half and then a quarter)

1 tomato

1 handful of washed and dried baby spinach (I buy 'washed and ready')

1 avocado - mashed (sprinkled with salt – optional)

Method

1. Make sure your vegetables are washed and clean. Cut tomato into quarters but not completely so it still holds together. Set aside on a plate.

Poached Egg -On the hob - Make sure your eggs are really fresh.

1. Crack your egg into a bowl or onto a saucer, this makes it easier to slide into the pan. If there is any very runny white surrounding the thicker white then tip this away.

2. Fill a pot with water, at least 5cm deep. Add a drop of vinegar to the water and bring to a simmer. Don't add any salt as this may break up the egg white. Stir the water to create a gentle whirlpool to help the egg white wrap around the yolk.

3. Slowly tip the egg into the centre. Make sure the heat is low enough not to throw the egg around – there should only be small bubbles rising.

4. Cook for 3-4 minutes or until the white is set.

5. Lift the egg out with a slotted spoon and drain it on kitchen paper. Trim off any straggly bits of white. If you need to cook more than one poached egg, keep it at the right temperature in warm water, but make sure the water isn't hot enough to overcook the egg.

Serving suggestion:
Serve on bed of avocado and tortilla. Season with black pepper and chopped chives if so desired.

Back from work - poached egg but 1
Poached Egg on Avocado Mash

Serves 1

1 slice of wholemeal bread
2 eggs
1 pickled or boiled
  beetroot
A handful of spinach
6 baby plum or cherry
  tomatoes
A handful of cheddar
  cheese - cubed, **or feta
  cheese** - crumbled
½ of 1 medium sized
  avocado
A pinch of salt
A grind of black pepper

Trying to incorporate some iron
into my dinner, but keeping it
quick and easy...it might be a
breakfast choice for some but I
would eat it at any time of day.

Method

1. Rinse and dry spinach with a kitchen towel and place on one half of a dinner plate.

2. Cut 3 pickled beetroots into quarters place on spinach.

3. Rinse the tomatoes and leave them whole to add to the rest of the salad. Crumble some feta cheese over it (optional). (I didn't have feta that evening, extra mature cheddar had to do. It was nice, but it wasn't quite the same)

4. Rinse and dry avocado. Cut in half, remove the stone and scoop out the flesh.

5. Mash avocado with a fork and season with a pinch of Himalayan salt and a grind or two of black pepper and put to the side.

6. Poach two eggs. (Alas! One of the eggs didn't make it!!) Pop bread in the toaster.

7. When toast is ready top with avocado mash and poached eggs.

It makes a very filling meal! Bon Appetit!

This recipe will remain forever special to me. It is dedicated to all those special people who cared and provided for me and mine, and community at large during that unprecedented global pandemic. There he was all 6ft 5in of him behind a mask, 'placing this adapted pizza on my car. He found a box for it as well!

If you Haven't got a Cousin Like Mine...

Serves 1 or 2 (if served with a salad)

1 Naan bread
1 egg
½ green bell pepper - sliced
¼ chopped red onion
1 chopped chorizo
3 tbsp tomato ketchup
A pinch of black pepper
A pinch of chilli flakes (optional)
¼ tsp of mixed herb
A handful rated cheddar cheese or mozzarella (he made it with mozzarella. I only had cheddar)

Method

1. Heat the oven to 180°C (conventional oven 160°C if fan-assisted oven).

2. Spread the ketchup over the Naan.

3. Season with black pepper, chilli flakes and mixed herbs.

4. Break 1 egg over the ketchup.

5. Scatter sliced chorizo, onions and green over.

6. Top with grated cheese

7. Place in the top of the oven and bake for 15 minutes or until cheese melted and egg cooked through.

Serving suggestion:
Serve with a side green salad/carrot batons and cucumber sticks.

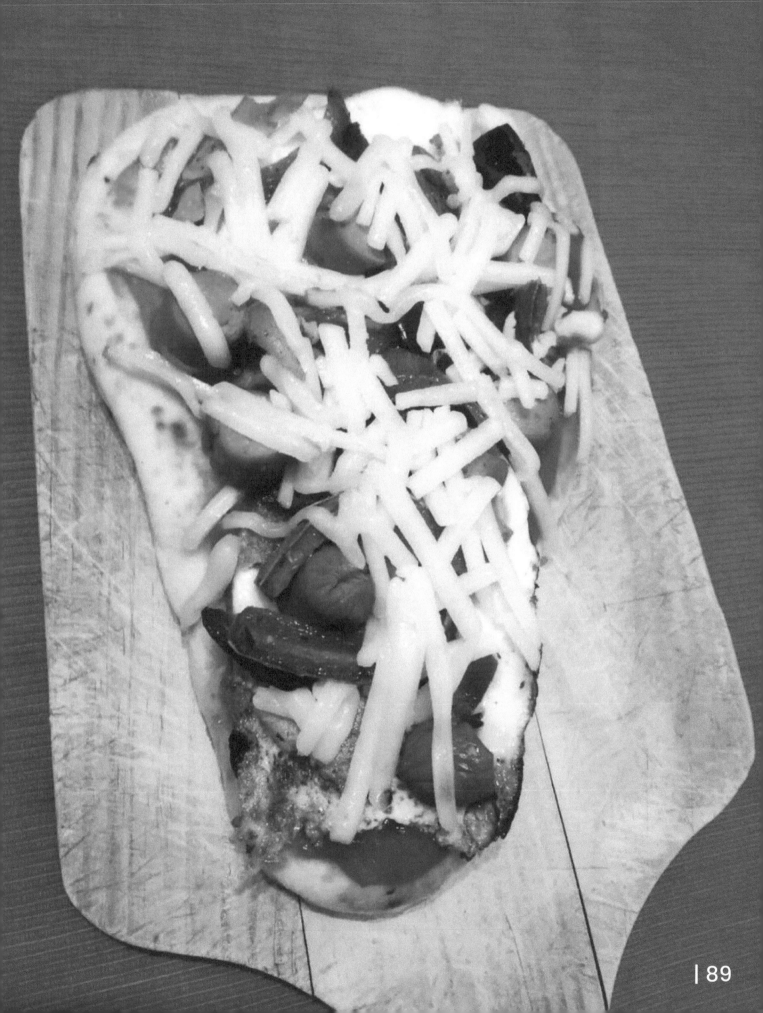

Crunchy Tuna Wrap ——————————

Serves 1
1 wholemeal wrap
A handful of iceberg lettuce or little gem lettuce
2 small chilli pickled gherkins (about 2.5 inches long) - sliced and chopped
1/5 of a cucumber - cut lengthways and seeds scooped out
¼ of a red onion - finely chopped
1 can of tuna in sunflower oil – drain
1 tbsp light mayonnaise
¼ tsp freshly ground black pepper
1 slice of red bell pepper - finely chopped

Method

1. In a bowl mash tuna, add mayonnaise and black pepper. Mix well. Add in vegetables and stir properly.

2. Heat the wrap in the microwave for 10 seconds.

3. Lay lettuce in the wrap and add crunchy tuna filling.

Serving suggestion:
Serve with a side salad.

Chicken & Salsa Wrap

Serves 1

For chicken:

2 chicken breasts - cut into strips, (you don't need two, but I make more than I need to have cold in a salad or another wrap the next day)
2 tsp sunflower oil
1 tsp garlic granules
¼ tsp salt
1 tsp freshly ground black pepper

Tomato salsa:

1 onion - chopped
2 cloves of garlic - minced
4 fresh red tomatoes - chopped
1 red chilli - chopped (or chilli flakes will work if you don't have fresh chilli)
15 ml olive oil
Juice of ½ a lime (optional)
½ tsp of sugar (optional)
Salt and black pepper - to taste
½ tsp of fresh parsley

Method

Tomato Salsa:

1. Heat oil over low to medium heat. Add onions and fry for 1 minute. Add garlic and fry for another minute.

2. Add chopped tomatoes and fresh chilli and season with salt and sugar (if using).
   The sugar accentuates the flavour of the tomatoes). Add 20ml of water. Lower heat, replace lid and allow to simmer for 10 minutes.

3. Add black pepper and parsley. Stir and turn off heat.

Chicken:

1. Season chicken strips with salt, garlic granules and black pepper.

2. Heat oil in a pan and add the chicken.

3. Stir fry chicken for 4 mins. Check with a skewer to ensure it is cooked through.

Serving suggestion:

If having it hot – heat up one wrap in the microwave for 10 seconds before serving

If cold – just get on with it.....

Chicken Avocado Smash Wrap

Serves 1

1 large ripe avocado
A squeeze of lemon juice
¼ tsp ground black pepper
A large pinch of salt
3 leaves of little gem lettuce
1 spring onion - sliced
¼ tsp of garlic granules
2 chicken breasts

Method

1. Cut avocado in half. Remove stone and peel off the skin. Mash avocado. Squeeze in a little lemon. Stir and set aside.

2. Shred lettuce leaves and put to one side.

Ensure to keep chicken preparation area and utensils and separate from the vegetable preparation areas.

3. Mix black pepper, salt and garlic granules and season chicken.

4. Heat the oil in a frying pan then add the chicken breasts and allow to cook for 2-3 minutes or until brown.

5. Turn the chicken over and cover and allow to cook on the other side for 7-8 minutes or until cooked through. Check the inside is cooked by poking with the tip of sharp knife – the juices should run clear. If not, keep cooking for another minute or so and check again. Rest for 5 minutes before serving. (This helps the chicken reabsorb the juices so the chicken isn't dry)

6. Slice chicken breast. If desired, spread mayonnaise on wrap, load with lettuce first, mashed avocado, chicken and spring onion. Fold wrap and enjoy.

Falafel

Serves 1

400g chickpeas
2 dessert spoons of plain flour
Zest from one lemon
2 tbsp water
1 tsp ground cumin
½ tsp salt
1 tsp freshly ground black pepper
4 tsp sunflower oil
1 large garlic clove - finely chopped
½ tsp chilli powder (omit if serving with a hot salsa)

Serving suggestion:
Serve in a wrap with hot salsa sauce, or with some salad and yoghurt in pitta bread or with couscous and salsa. You've got options.

Method

1. Drain the can of chickpeas and put in a colander. Rinse under running water.

2. Place the chickpeas in a saucepan and mash with a potato masher or blend with a hand blender (my preference)until as smooth as possible.

3. Add the cumin, garlic, lemon zest, flour and salt. Season with black pepper and mix well with a wooden spoon (I tend to be generous with the black pepper. Add the chilli powder if using.

4. Using your hands, form the mixture into 6 – 9 equal-sized balls and flatten slightly if serving in a burger or pitta bread. Alternatively scoop with an ice cream scoop or tablespoon and flatten when placed in the pan.

5. Heat 2 teaspoons of the oil to a frying pan over a low heat. Add falafel balls and cook for 4 minutes. Flip onto the other side and add 2 teaspoons of oil to the pan. Cook for a further 3–4 minutes, or until golden brown and crisp on both sides.

Hummus

1 can chickpeas - drained
Lemon juice – from one
  lemon, ½ zested
60ml cold water
1 small garlic clove -peeled
and crushed
3 tbsp tahini
1 tbsp olive oil - to garnish
½ tsp freshly ground
  black pepper

Serving suggestion:
Serve with
breadstick/crudites/ or as a
spread in a vegetable wrap

Method

1. Rinse the chickpeas under cold running water and strain using a sieve or colander. Place the chickpeas and water in a food processor and blitz – only slightly smooth.

2. Add lemon juice, tahini and garlic and blitz again.

3. Test the consistency – I don't like it too thick. Gradually add a little more water – maximum 30ml. You don't want it runny. Add lemon zest and blitz lightly until silky smooth or until the hummus is smooth and silky.

4. Season with a pinch of sea salt and transfer to a bowl with a sealable lid. Swirl the top of the hummus with the back of a dessert spoon and drizzle over a little olive oil.

Akara

2 cups of black eyed beans - whole or broken. Broken beans van be purchased from most African grocery stores.

1½ scotch bonnet pepper - diced

1 red onion - chopped

1 tbsp of ground crayfish (optional)

1 Bouillon cube (optional)

Sunflower oil for frying

Akara is made from blended black- eyed beans. It is usually served at breakfast and sometimes at dinner in many parts of Nigeria. It is so popular that is fried and sold by many street vendors. A lot of families tend to buy from the street vendors in order to save on time and effort.

Method

1. Soak beans in a bowl of water for about 30 minutes or till the skin gradually swells.

2. Peel the skin by rubbing the beans by hand (similar to doing the laundry by hand). Alternatively, transfer to a blender and pulse about twice to split the beans. If using broken beans you would neither need to rub vigorously nor pulse in a blender. You would only need to rinse it a few times to get rid of the skin.

3. Rinse a few times to rid the beans of the skin. Blend the peeled beans with half of pepper and onion, crayfish, salt and bouillon powder (or cube). Half a cup of water should do. Try to keep water to a minimum, otherwise you will end up with a watery mixture and flat oil-sodden Akara. We don't want that. Do we?!

4. Whisk the batter to incorporate air. The batter should become fluffy. An electric whisk takes about a minute to two. In the absence of a whisk, continuously stir with a wooden spoon. Stir in remaining diced onions and pepper.

Continued on page 102.

Akara continued...

I dedicate this recipe to my mother of blessed memory. She always made this herself. Living in the UK, she didn't have the option of the street vendor. Long before the advent of 'broken beans' my mum would soak the black eyed beans at night and wake up at the crack of dawn to prepare Akara. When I lived at home as a young adult, I was never a morning person. However, my mum knew just the way to chase away the morning blues – a knock on my door and voila! Piping hot akara served with a bowl of steaming cornflour porridge (her adaptation of the Nigerian Ogi (pap) served on my favourite red plastic tray. Bless her soul.)

5. Add oil to a pot/sauté pan/frying pan over medium heat. Check for readiness by adding a pinch of salt. If it sizzles the oil is hot enough to start frying. Using a spoon, scoop little balls about 1.5 inch in diameter into the hot oil and fry until golden brown and turning over half way through.

6. When brown and a little crispy on both sides, use a slotted spoon to remove from the pan and drain on greaseproof paper or kitchen towel.

Serving suggestion:
Serve with ogi, custard or bread. Akara is no less scrumptious if served on its own.

Seafood Dishes

After the long commute, the last thing on my mind is a complicated meal...No matter how simple I've got to keep it healthy – A slab of protein, two portions of vegetable, and some plantain which is technically classed as a fruit, but cooked and eaten like a vegetable. Whatever its classification, it is a favourite of mine.

grilled Seabass
& the Least Likely Bedfellows

Serves 1
For the fish:
1 fillet of seabass
½ tsp coarsely ground
  black pepper
A pinch of salt
¼ tsp dried Italian
  herbs or fresh parsley

Vegetables:
A handful of mangetout -
rinsed
½ courgette - rinsed and
cut into quarters
½ plantain (nearly ripe) -
peeled and cut into quarters
½ garlic clove - crushed
½ tsp mixed herbs
½ tbsp olive oil

Method
1. Heat oven to 200°C

2. Place plantain on greaseproof parchment or foil – (place on a large baking leaving space for other items) rub olive oil on plantain and place in the oven.

3. Rub courgette with oil and a pinch of mixed herbs and place on parchment paper.

4. In a cup, mix garlic, olive oil, salt, and black pepper. Place fish in a shallow ovenproof glass or ceramic baking dish and rub fish with oil mixture.

5. When the plantain has been in the oven for 5 mins, place fish, uncovered in the oven to bake.

6. When the fish has been in the oven for 5 mins, place courgettes in the oven.

7. When the fish has been in the oven for a further 5 minutes, sprinkle with parsley or Italian seasoning and leave to bake for 5 more minutes (or until the thickest part of the fish flakes easily, if baking a whole fish).

8. Place mangetout in a steamer and steam for 5 – 7 mins (I prefer them al dente).

Serving suggestion:
Serve with a side of tomato stew or a drizzle of chilli oil.

I would usually ask the fishmonger to cut some of my fish into steaks after scaling and cleaning it. It saves me a job when I am grilling for one or two. I would grill one and save the rest. If cooking for 4, I would grill a very large one. I still do a final wash and scrape in case they missed any scales.

Grilled Plantain
with Grilled Tilapia & Stew

Serves 1

1 tilapia steak - cleaned

½ clove of garlic - minced

1 sprig of thyme - chopped

 A pinch of salt (I use Himalayan salt)

1/4 tsp ground black pepper

½ - 1 ripe plantain - sliced diagonally

Method

1. Heat oven at 200°C.

2. Rinse tilapia steak and pat dry. Make two slashes into the skin on each side of the fish. Rub garlic and thyme into the slashes in the skin.

3. Place steak in one section of the baking dish and place plantain in the other section.

4. Bake 15-20 minutes until the fish flakes easily with a fork. Prod plantain with a fork; it should feel firm, and not wet when cooked.

TIPS FOR COOKING TILAPIA

The first step to cook a whole fish, whether you get your fish frozen like I did or fresh from a tank, is to make sure your tilapia is scaled and thoroughly cleaned. Ask the fishmonger if you're not sure.

The Seabass Belleful
with Stewed Vegetables

Serves 4

4 whole sea bass - about 400g each scaled and gutted

80ml olive oil

1½ lemons

1 tbsp chopped oregano

2 tbsp chopped parsley

1 tsp salt

2 tsp ground black pepper

Stewed vegetables:

1 sweet potato - washed peeled and cut into one inch pieces

150g sliced curly kale - washed

2 medium carrots - washed and cut into 1-inch pieces

1 large bell pepper - cut into 1-inch squares

½ tsp chilli flakes

Tomato stew (page 38)

6 broccoli florets - cut in half

4 cauliflower florets - cut in half

Method

1. Heat grill at 170°C (I have an oven with a grill function – if using a standalone grill heat at medium).

2. Brush each fish all over with about ½ tbsp olive oil and season with salt and black pepper, inside and out.

3. Squeeze quarter of one lemon into a bowl with the remaining olive oil and herbs and rub on the insides of the fish.

4. Grill on each side for 6 minutes until the skin is golden and the white flesh flakes easily.

Stewed vegetables:

1. Bring one cup of water to boil.

2. Add the sweet potato and allow to simmer for 3 minutes and switch off heat.

3. Heat tomato stew, stir in chilli flakes and 2 bay leaves.

4. Add sweet potato and carrots to simmering stew. Allow to simmer for 2 minutes. Add broccoli, kale and pepper and allow to simmer for 2 minutes.

5. Mash a few pieces of the sweet potato to thicken the mixture. Stir and allow to cook for another minute.

6. Turn off heat, replace lid and allow to stand for 1 minute before serving.

7. Remove bay leaves before serving.

Sauteéd Potatoes & Jewelled Salmon —

Serves 4

3 Maris Piper potatoes
1tsp Olive oil or sunflower oil
4 salmon fillets
2 tbsp pomegranate molasses (I didn't have pomegranate molasses on this occasion I used honey)
1 inch of ginger - rinsed and grated
1 tbsp olive oil
½ lime - juiced
1 pomegranate - seeds only

Method

1. Cut potatoes into chunks. Bring a large pan of water to the boil, then cook the potatoes for 3 mins. Drain and place on a tray lined with paper towel and leave to cool.

2. Put the salmon skin-side down on a large baking sheet. Mix the pomegranate molasses or honey, grated ginger, ½ tbsp olive oil and half the lime juice with a good pinch of salt and a few grinds of black pepper in a small bowl, then brush the mixture all over the flesh of the salmon. Chill for at least 20 mins.

3. Heat the oven to 200°C.

4. Bake the salmon, uncovered, for 10-12 mins, until cooked through. Check this by poking a knife into the fillet and ensuring the fish flakes easily.

5. Heat 6-8 tbsp sunflower or olive oil in a large non-stick frying pan until you can feel a strong heat rising. Turn the heat to medium-high, so that the potatoes sizzle, but don't stir until they start to brown underneath.

6. Turn the potatoes all evenly 2 or 3 times until nicely browned all over – this can take about 7 mins. Then lift out with a fish slice or large slotted spoon to drain on more kitchen towel.

Sweet Chilli Salmon & Quinoa Medley

Serves 1

1 salmon fillet
1 tbsp sweet chilli sauce
1 tsp lemon juice
1 garlic clove
1 tsp soy sauce
Coriander/parsley/basil to serve

½ **cup quinoa** - rinsed and drained
¼ **tin chickpeas** - rinsed and drained
⅓ **cup couscous**
1 **cup of vegetable stock**

My teenage daughter grilled the salmon, plated the food and served it up with so much love and consideration for her tired mum. I was so grateful.
I didn't have the heart to say "Baby, never serve salmon with Rioja" Lol!

Method

1. Heat an oven at 200°C.

2. Bring vegetable stock to the boil. Follow cooking instructions on packet for quinoa. After 10 minutes add the chickpeas. Turn off the heat and stir in the couscous. The steam will cook the couscous.

3. Make the glaze: Combine sweet chilli sauce, lemon juice and soy sauce in a measuring jug or bowl.

4. Glaze and bake the salmon: Line an ovenproof dish with parchment paper and add the salmon, skin-side down. Generously spread the glaze over and place the salmon in hot oven for 7-10 minutes until sticky and cooked to your preference.

Serving suggestion(s):
Drizzle glaze over the dish and serve with a green salad

Kale, Sweet Potato & Hake

Serves 1

1 hake fillet

1 medium sized sweet potato - scrubbed, peeled or unpeeled and cut into ¼ even strips

½ tsp smoked paprika

2 tbsp olive oil or sunflower oil

½ tsp salt

½ tsp black pepper

½ tsp garlic granules

½ tbsp cornflour

Method

1. Soak the potato strips in cold water for at least 30 minutes (optional step but highly recommended because it removes excess starch and allows for better crispiness. I tend to soak in the morning. It's fine to soak them overnight).

2. Heat oven and baking tray to 220°C.

3. Dry strips with a clean napkin to remove excess moisture. Coat strips with oil, cornflour, salt and spices. Ensure strips are evenly coated.

4. Place on baking tray and bake for 15 mins. Turn them over half way through.

5. When cooked through, remove from oven and leave to stand at room temperature. Cover with paper towel to keep warm and crisp.

6. Serve with mayo or any dip of your choice.

To oven roast the hake fillet:

1. Reduce the oven heat to 180 C. Rinse and dry hake with kitchen towel. Coat with sunflower oil. Season with salt, onion powder and black pepper.

2. Roast for 8 – 10 minutes. When cooked it should be flaky and opaque.

Let's Keep it Green Shall We ————

Serves 1

1 salmon steak
- about 1" thick
1/4 tsp sea salt
1/2 tsp freshly ground
black pepper
2 tbsp olive oil

Method

1. Preheat oven to 200°C. Season both sides of salmon steak with sea salt and pepper.

2. Heat a grill pan on high heat for 90 seconds. Turn heat down to medium, add olive oil and then add steak.

3. Cook each side for 3-4 minutes until seared and golden. Place in the oven for five minutes. Remove from oven, allow to rest for a few minutes and serve over greens.

Greens:

Reference: Just When you thought Kale couldn't Party (on page 16, Steps 1 – 4), leaving out the carrots.

Oven-baked Sweet Potato
With Mackerel Stew & Avocado

Serves 1

1 sweet potato
1 tsp salt
1 tsp freshly ground
black pepper
½ tsp ground chilli
 powder
A knob of butter
2 pieces of clean fresh
mackerel or 1 can of
 mackerel

Serving Suggestion:
Accompany with a salad.

Tip:
*Canned mackerel is a good
alternative.*

Method

1. Heat oven to 220°C.

2. Season mackerel pieces with salt and chilli powder and place in a small, lined baking tray – bake for 10 minutes.

3. Wash sweet potato thoroughly, pat dry and pierce 3-4 times with a fork and place potato on microwave-safe plate and microwave (800 watts) for 5 minutes.

4. If the potato isn't fork tender after 5 minutes, microwave again for 30 seconds. If you like to eat the skin, melt a small knob of butter over the potato rub some sea salt and black pepper over it. Place potato on a baking tray lined with parchment paper and bake in the oven for 10 minutes. This should make the skin crispy. If eating without the skin, split the baked potato down the middle and scoop out the potato flesh.

Mackerel Stew:

1. Heat up 2 ladles of tomato stew (page 38) and add 2 pieces of mackerel. Flake the mackerel in the stew and allow to simmer for 3 mins.

2. Serve.

Super Salad & Thyme Salmon _____

Serves 1

Thyme Salmon:
4 salmon fillets - skinned
3 tbsp extra virgin olive oil
2 garlic cloves - minced
1½ tsp kosher salt
½ tsp freshly ground
 black pepper
2 sprigs of fresh thyme
leaves
½ tsp paprika
Zest of ½ lemon

Super Salad:

4 large pickled beetroots -
quartered

1 small bag of baby
spinach - ready to use

A handful of pitted black
olives
1 small pack of cherry
 tomatoes - sliced in half
A handful feta cheese
1 tsp vinaigrette (optional)

Method

1. Heat oven to 200°C. Drizzle with olive oil and rub oil evenly into all of the salmon filets. Rub salt, paprika and pepper. Top with the crushed garlic and lemon zest all over the salmon. Rub thyme sprigs over the salmon and place on the salmon.

2. Line baking tray with greaseproof paper and place salmon in the tray and put in the heated oven.

3. Leave in the oven for 10 mins or until the salmon flakes easily with a fork.

4. Assemble super salad to your liking using the ingredients listed, if using vinaigrette drizzle over vegetables.

5. Crumble feta cheese over salad.

Uni Corner

My nephew got some advice at the start of university: "Make sure you know how to make stew. It can give you a minimum of 5 different meals for the week. Cook a large pot and freeze in jars. Use one jar per recipe." I continue to give that advice to young people of West African descent and beyond. Whenever you miss home cooking, with a jar of stew, you'll be just fine.

Enjoy:

Tomato Stew – see Page38

Bolognese

Chilli Con Carne

Okra and Stew

Rice and Stew

Beans and Dodo(fried or grilled plantain)

Spaghetti and Sardines

Rice & Stew as We Sabi

Serves 1

1 cup of rice – boil following pack instructions

Serve with stew (on page 38)

Method

As I try to incorporate more protein, but not compromising on flavour, I would occasionally jazz up my rice with some frozen peas and red lentils . I add the lentils to the rice at the start of the cooking and I add the frozen peas just a few minutes before the rice and lentils are cooked.

Bolognese - Uni Style

Serves 4

500g beef/turkey mince

1 medium onion - peeled and diced

2 sticks of celery - rinsed and diced

2 garlic cloves - peeled and finely chopped

½ tsp chilli powder

½ tsp dried oregano

½ ground black pepper

½ tsp paprika

½ tsp curry powder

1 beef bouillon cube

Tomato stew (page 38)

1 tbsp sunflower oil

½ tsp salt

1 medium carrot - peeled and chopped

I always put my pasta to boil first. Follow the pack instructions and you'll be fine.
Tip: Boil it al dente, don't drain all the liquid. Leave about 1 tablespoon in the pasta. Add few drops of olive oil to prevent it from sticking and a little ground black pepper and cover it for a few minutes for the pasta to absorb the flavours.

Method

1. Defrost frozen stew.

2. Place a medium sized pan on medium heat. Heat oil – do not allow to smoke. Fry onions for 3 minutes and add mince. Season with bouillon and spices and stir fry for 5 minutes.

3. Stir in stew depending on quantity required – enough for the consistency to drop off a spoon. Replace lid and leave to simmer for 5 minutes.

4. Add diced carrots and celery. Cover for 1 minute. Turn off heat. The steam will cook the carrots –you want them al dente.

Bolognese with a twist? Add 2 tablespoons of tomato ketchup

Fancy some variety?

Split Bolognese in two portions. Save half for **Chilli Con Carne**. *For Chilli Con Carne you only need to add ½ can of red kidney beans (rinsed). If you want your Chilli Con Carne hotter, add some more chilli powder and a ladle of stew.*

Stewed Beans & Dodo

For picture of Stewed Beans, see Let's Pack It All In - page 15

1 cup of black-eyed beans - rinsed
1 medium sized onion - peeled and diced
Tomato Stew (Page 38)
1 tsp spray oil
A pinch of salt

Dodo (fried/grilled plantain):
1 medium sized ripe plantain - peeled and sliced diagonally
Sunflower oil for frying

*I advise soaking the beans the night before as it softens them and cooks so much quicker.

Method

1. Soak Beans overnight or two hours in advance*. Alternatively, put a medium pot of water to . Add rinsed beans. Ensure the water is approx. 5cm above the beans.

2. Cover and allow to simmer on high heat. If boiling beans without soaking, allow to cook for 30 minutes. Check to see if you can mash with a fork. It should be as soft as baked beans. If pre-soaked, check in 20 mins. Add half the chopped onions, season with salt to your taste and allow to boil.

Dodo:

1. Heat oven to 200°C. Heat a baking tray.
2. In a bowl place sliced plantain and spray with oil. Toss thoroughly to ensure all plantain is coated with oil.

3. Take tray out of oven and line with grease proof paper. Lay out plantain – no overlapping and bake in oven for 25 mins – turning them over halfway through. If you have an air fryer, plantain will be ready in 15 minutes.

Back to our beans...

1. Heat a tbsp of oil and fry half the onions. Add stew about half the quantity of the beans. For a twist add two bay leaves to the stew mixture. Reheat on low heat for 3 – 5 minutes.

2. When the beans are soft, drain excess fluid and add the stew. Stir and reduce heat and allow to simmer for a further 5 minutes. Mash some of the beans if you like it very creamy. Remove bay leaves before serving.

Sardines & Spaghetti

Serves 1

1 can of sardines - drained (you could used canned mackerel, herring or any other canned fish)

1 tbsp olive oil

1 small onion (red or white) - chopped

10 cherry tomatoes - halved (alternatively half a can of chopped tomatoes – without the juice if you don't have fresh)

2 large cloves of garlic - chopped

200g wholemeal spaghetti

1 tsp chilli flakes

8 olives (green or black) - sliced

A handful of fresh parsley – if you don't have fresh 1 tsp of dried parsley will do

Method

1. Boil the spaghetti in hot salted water following pack instructions – drain with a colander when cooked – reserve some of the water for later.

2. Whilst the spaghetti is boiling, heat the oil in a saucepan, using a wooden spoon stir in onions and fry for two mins, add garlic and chilli flakes – stir for a couple of minutes.

3. Add tomatoes and slightly pressing with the back of the wooden spoon to release some of the juice.

4. Add sardines and olives – break up the sardine pieces with the wooden spoon.

5. Add the drained spaghetti and stir thoroughly, add the parsley.

6. Add a tablespoon of water reserved from the spaghetti, stir thoroughly and cover for 2 mins. Turn off heat.

Okra & Stew

10 **okra fingers** – washed, dried with a paper towel

2 handfuls of spinach – washed and chopped

1 tsp ground crayfish

¼ small red onion - chopped

1 cup of water

1 pinch of bouillon powder (optional)

1 pinch of salt

1 pinch of chilli flakes – adjust to taste

Method

1. Grate okra using the side with larger holes. Alternatively, chop okra into huge chunks – place in a blender with the water and pulse once or twice. You do not want to liquidise the okra.

2. In a small pot, put to boil. When water begins to boil, add chopped onions, allow to boil for 1 one minute. Add ground crayfish, salt and chilli flakes. Allow to cook for 2 minutes. Add grated okra, allow to cook for 1 minute.

3. Add spinach, reduce heat and allow to simmer for 2 minutes.

Serving suggestion:

Serve with chicken/beef/fish tomato stew and pounded yam (made following pack instructions) or mashed potato.

Rice Dishes

Three's Company with Curry Goat _____

Serves 2

1.4kg goat meat with bone cut medium-sized
or (1kg if boneless)
6 tbsp curry powder
1 inch of grated ginger
1 large onion - diced
4 garlic cloves - peeled and
 crushed
1 scotch bonnet pepper -
 thinly sliced
A pinch of salt

Curry Sauce:
4-5 tbsp sunflower oil
1 sprig of fresh thyme
4 cups of boiling water
1 tbsp tomato puree
1 onion medium onion -
 finely chopped
2 medium potatoes -
 peeled and largely cut
Salt and black pepper to
 taste

Three's Company:
¾ cup brown basmati rice
¾ cup tri-colour quinoa
¾ cup couscous (I would
 substitute with frozen garden
 peas on the days I have my
 eye on the carb intake)

Method

Meat prep:

1. In a large mixing bowl combine the goat meat along with curry powder, chopped onions and crushed garlic, salt and scotch bonnet pepper.

2. Mix well and cover. Leave at room temperature for 3 hours/or in the refrigerator for a minimum of 5-6 hours, or preferably overnight.

Curry sauce:

1. Once the meat has marinated sufficiently, take it out from the refrigerator (if placed in the fridge) and remove the onions and scotch bonnet peppers from it and set aside.
2. In a large saucepan, heat the sunflower oil. Once the oil is sufficiently hot, put in the marinated meat and brown it on both sides, keep turning over and stirring.

3. As the meat turns brown, add the thyme and pour in the hot water. Add the chopped onion and the scotch bonnet peppers and onions saved from the marinade. Cover with a lid and leave to cook for 10 minutes.
(Adjust spices to taste. Increase the amount of curry if you like it really strong).

4. After 10 minutes add the cut potatoes along with the tomato puree and allow to cook over reduced heat for 40 minutes or until the meat is thoroughly cooked.

5. Once ready, remove the scotch bonnet and serve hot.

Three's Company:

1. Wash rice in very hot water till it runs clear. Following pack instructions put to boil adding a little piece of vegetable stock cube (my chosen brand of rice boils for 22 mins).

2. 10 minutes in, rinse quinoa and add to boiling rice and stir. You may need to add 20 mill of water. Cook for a further 10 mins.

3. If using coucous, add the coucous and cook for 2 mins and turn off the heat. The steam will cook the coucous. Ready to serve in 3 minutes.

Serving suggestion:

Serve curry goat with Three's Company and any vegetable of your choice – I had red cabbage in the fridge. I steamed that alongside some radish. Enjoy!

If you don't fancy three's company serve with white rice.

Fun Fact: *Three's Company started out as a lucky combination of leftovers that just worked!*

Why not give the takeaway a miss this Friday?

Prawn & Egg Fried Rice

Serves 4

250g basmati rice

2 tbsp vegetable oil

2 garlic cloves - finely chopped

1 red chilli - deseeded and shredded

2 eggs - beaten

1 bunch spring onions - finely sliced

285g pack of cooked prawns

1 tbsp soy sauce (plus extra for serving - optional)

Method

1. Boil the rice following pack instructions (I tend to freestyle on my rice which may not work for everyone).

2. Heat the oil in a wok or large frying pan – medium heat. Add the garlic and chilli, then cook for 10 secs – do not let it burn (the garlic will taste bitter if it burns).

3. Add the cooked rice, stir fry for 1 min,

then push to the side of the pan. Pour the eggs into the empty side of the pan, then scramble them, stirring. As the eggs set, stir in the spring onions into the rice and egg, then cook for 2 mins until the peas are tender.

Add the prawns and soy sauce and give it all a good stir. Heat through, then serve with extra soy sauce on the side, if you like.

For extra veg – *why not throw in some frozen peas with the spring onions?*

Green Lentil Curry & Yellow Rice

2 tbsp sunflower oil

2 medium onions - cut into rough wedges

4 tbsp curry paste (Here's a tip – make your own: recipe on page 138 (I have tried most brands....if using ready made – I'll suggest a little more curry, cumin, ginger and chilli powder)

850ml vegetable stock

750g stewpack frozen vegetables

100g red lentils

200g basmati rice (I eat brown rice)

1 tsp turmeric

A handful of raisins and a handful roughly chopped parsley

Method

1. Heat the oil in a large pan. Add the onions and cook over a high heat for 5 minutes or until they are golden brown. Stir in the curry paste and cook for a minute. Slowly pour in a little of the stock so it sizzles, scraping any bits from the bottom of the pan. Gradually pour in the rest of the stock.

2. Add the lentils and leave to simmer for a further 15 minutes.

3. Separately, following pack instructions cook the rice, adding turmeric to the cooking water. Now get back to your curry.

4. Stir the frozen vegetables into the lentil mix, cover and simmer for 5 minutes or until the vegetables and lentils are cooked.

5. Season with salt, toss in some chopped parsley and a handful of raisins and serve immediately with the rice.

For a little colour and extra protein, I topped with a poached egg.

On a cold winter's evening reheat the left overs adding a little water and eat as a soup, on its own or with a piece of naan bread.

Curry Paste - bonus

We're going to need coriander seeds, cumin seeds, black peppercorns and fennel seeds. For colour and some heat, add a few dried red chillis.

Heat a frying pan over low heat and add the spices. Toast the spices very slowly without burning them. Make sure you break the red chilies into smaller pieces so they'll toast along with other dried spices. Keep tossing them to prevent burned spots. Once the spices are toasted, leave to cool completely.

When toasted spices are cool, place in a food processor and grind to a fine powder. Toasting releases the flavour of the spices. Add ginger, garlic, chopped shallots, ground turmeric, paprika, red chili powder, salt, tomato paste and white vinegar to the food processor.

Wash a jar and sterilise with hot water. When jar cools, scoop in curry paste. Cover with a layer of olive oil it should keep in the fridge for at least 3 months.

Egg Dishes

Eggie - Veggie Hash

Serves 1

2 large florets of cauliflower - chopped
¼ green pepper - chopped
¼ red pepper - chopped
¼ of a small onion
1 pinch of salt to taste
3 cherry tomatoes - sliced
½ small scotch bonnet pepper - chopped
2 large eggs - beaten
1 tbsp sunflower oil
A double pinch of ground black pepper

Method

1. Heat oil in a non-stick frying pan. Add onions and fry for 2 mins. Add sliced tomatoes and fry for 1 min. Add chopped cauliflower and peppers and fry for 2 mins, stirring throughout.

2. Season beaten eggs with salt and pour into the vegetable mix.

3. Stir with a fork as you would scrambled eggs for 2 mins or until cooked.

4. Season with a grind of black pepper.

5. I would add a tablespoon of tomato stew, but it really doesn't need it. I just love stew.

Serving suggestion:
Serve with a super salad (pages 42). It is quite filling on its own. If you want a more substantial meal, add boiled yam, boiled sweet potato or oven baked sweet potato fries.

Being Nigerian by origin and upbringing, Yam and eggs were a staple in most homes. Some homes had it for breakfast on a Saturday morning, whilst some had it as a quick fix for dinner. As I have grown older and tried to incorporate more vegetables into my diet, I bring you:

Fried yam, vegeomelette and caulijollof
Yam & Eggs with a Twist

Serves 1

Caulijollof:

1 ladleful of tomato stew.
Do you remember Tomato Stew from page 38? Yes, that one.

¼ tsp of curry powder

A pinch of dried thyme

¼ tsp of ground chilli powder

¼ tsp of dried chives

A pinch of salt

Half of a red onion -
chopped

1 tbsp olive oil

A small head of cauliflower
- grated

Method

1. Heat the olive oil on low heat and fry the chopped onions for just under two minutes.

2. Add stew, seasoning and stir. Leave on low heat for about a minute and a half. Some may break a little piece of a chicken stock cube for some more flavour.

3. Stir in grated cauliflower and dried chives. Cover with lid and allow to steam for 3 minutes.

4. If it tastes a little dry, add a little more stew and leave for a further minute.

5. Serve as an accompaniment to yam or serve as mains with some grilled chicken, grilled fish or stewed beef and a salad.

On a Saturday morning, I woke up craving a sardine or mackerel omelette - just the way my dad used to make it on Saturday mornings. He made the perfect 3-fold omelette. I am not there yet. In its place I decided on some eggs and some fried sweet potato. I always loved sweet and chilli. The plan was 3 slices of fried sweet potato and an omelette with tomatoes and scotch bonnet peppers. Half an hour later, this is what emerged!

Spinach Omelette
& Sweet Potato Medley

Serves 1
2 eggs
5 small plum tomatoes sliced in half
A pinch of chilli flakes
A pinch of salt
½ tsp ground black pepper
20 ml dairy milk/plant based milk
¼ small onion - chopped
¼ of a large sweet potato - diced
¼ green pepper - diced
¼ red pepper - diced
A large handful of baby spinach - rinsed and dried with a kitchen towel
Spray oil
¼ garlic - crushed
½ tsp grated ginger
1 tbsp sunflower oil for frying

Method

1. Heat oven at 200°C and line a baking tray with greaseproof paper.

2. Place cubed sweet potato in baking tray and spray with oil. Season with salt and black pepper place in the oven and set timer for 20 mins. (I wrote this before I bought an air fryer – 10 mins).

3. Arrange spinach on a dinner plate.

4. Whisk eggs add salt, a twist of ground black pepper and a pinch of chilli flakes. Continue to whisk and gradually add the milk. Stir in sliced tomatoes and onions.

5. Heat a tablespoon of oil in the frying pan, add crushed garlic. Fry for 30 seconds only.

6. Pour in the egg, ensure tomatoes and onions are evenly distributed in the mixture. In 2 minutes, turn down the heat and cover with a lid for the egg to set.

7. Stir fry grated ginger in a wok for one minute, add diced peppers and baked sweet potato and toss for 2 minutes. Turn off heat.

8. Using a spatula, remove the egg from the pan and place on the spinach. Top with stir fried peppers and potato medley and serve immediately.

We Had it All
- Fried Yam, Avocado & Poached Egg

Serves 1

Yam cut into chips
½ avocado
½ tsp paprika
A handful of rocket leaves
Sunflower oil for frying

To serve: 1 tbsp Shito - Ghanaian pepper sauce

Poached egg:
1 tbsp white vinegar
1 free-range egg
A pinch of salt and freshly ground black pepper

Method

1. Heat sunflower oil over medium heat. Lower heat, add yam chips and fry for 10 mins. Turning over half way through. Chips should be fork tender when ready.

Alternatively, toss raw yam chips with minimal spray oil and place in the air fryer set at 200C for 15 mins or a fan assisted oven for 25 mins.

2. Fill a small pan just over one third full with cold water and bring it to the boil.

3. Add the vinegar and turn down to simmer.

4. Crack the egg into a small bowl and gently tip into the simmering water. Lightly poach for 2-3 minutes.

4. Remove with a slotted spoon and drain on a kitchen towel.

5. Season with salt and freshly ground black pepper and serve immediately.

Breakfast on a Saturday morning after my workout. It rocks at dinner too. Some protein and a rich source of potassium.

Spinach Omelette
with Bacon, Broccoli and Mushroom Hash

Spinach Omelette (page 144)

3 brocolli florets - sliced
2 rashers of bacon (smoked or unsmoked) – chopped – or you can buy bacon bits
5 mushrooms - sliced
½ red onion - chopped
Double pinch of ground black pepper

Method

1. Heat a medium sized frying pan. Add bacon bits and onions to fry, stirring with a wooden spoon for about two minutes.

2. Reduce flame to low. Add mushrooms and broccoli.

3. Season with black pepper.

4. Stir for another 3 minutes. Turn off the heat and serve immediately.

Sweet Treats

For elevenses today I fancied a lemon cheesecake.. Or just something sweet.... No, it was a lemon cheesecake I wanted.

I adapted the traditional recipe so quickly and this baby was ready in 15 mins! I was so embarrassed at my speed and innovation! There are all the arguments for and against artificial sweeteners. I think if I have it a couple of times a year, I'll be fine.

Reduced Sugar Lemon Cheesecake
On the Easy

Serves 1

1½ tbsp lowest fat cream cheese

½ tsb granulated sweetener

1 tbsp lemon juice

1 pinch of grated lemon rind

For the base:
2 digestive biscuits
1 tsp olive spread

Method

1. Wrap digestive biscuits in greaseproof paper and crush with a rolling pin.

2. Place olive spread in a ramekin and melt in the microwave for 3 seconds or until runny.

3. Stir biscuit crumbs and scoop into a dessert bowl and press firmly into the bottom of the dessert bowl (you can leave it in the ramekin if you do not have a dessert bowl). Place in the coldest part of your fridge (I placed it in the freezer – I only had time for a coffee break).

4. In another ramekin, whisk the cream cheese with the sweetener to incorporate some air add the lemon juice, a little pinch of lemon rind.

5. Spread over the base, sprinkle another pinch of grated lemon rind over the top and return to the freezer for another 5 mins to set. If you are not in a hurry place in the fridge for a couple of hours – Enjoy!

Have you ever woken up and fancied something decadent, but your voice of reason whispered "Come on buddy, not now!"? I woke up craving blueberry cheesecake...and this was birthed...Enjoy with minimal guilt. It's packed with protein – throw in some chia seeds. You can't go wrong with this.

Cheesecake - No Cheese! _____

1½ biscuits of Protein Weetabix (any brand wheat biscuits will do)
3 heaped tbsp of Greek style yogurt or Greek yogurt
1 handful of blueberries
1.5 tsp organic honey (adjust quantity to taste)
1 tbsp virgin olive oil

Variations:
Crank it up a notch – why not add some chia seeds to the yogurt?

Or for some crunch, sprinkle mixed seeds and nuts over it?

Method
1. On a chopping board gently crush the Weetabix with a rolling pin.

2. In a bowl mix the crushed Weetabix with the olive oil and place in a small ceramic dish (a small baking tray will do). Press down with a tablespoon.

3. Scoop the yoghurt over it and spread with the spoon. Place in the fridge to set.

4. To make blueberry compote: Rinse blueberries and place in a small pot over low heat and mash with a potato masher for about 2 mins. Add one tablespoon of water, stir for 1 min.

5. Add honey and keep stirring with a wooden spoon for 4 mins.

6. Remove from heat and pour into a ramekin. Put some ice-cold water (about 1cm high) in a cereal bowl and place the ramekin in it to cool for about 5 mins.

7. Spread compote over the yoghurt and Weetabix and enjoy!

Every now and then, I fancy something sweet after a meal. These are quick and easy to make, thus very convenient. I once took a tray of these to a party, and just like magic, the tray was empty within minutes!

Little Cups of Sweet Delight ——————

Serves 6

Lemon Curd
1 handful of blueberries
2 kiwi fruit - chopped into tiny pieces
Caster sugar (optional)
(Alternatively you can use other fruit such as raspberries and strawberries)
18 mini pastry cases

Method

1. Set mini pastry cases out on two trays. In each cup place, ¼ teaspoon of lemon curd.

2. In one tray, add 3 blueberries in each cup and press down lightly.

3. In the other tray, place a heaped teaspoon of chopped kiwi fruit.

4. Sprinkle some icing sugar over each cup (optional).

Index

A big *thank you to...*

Creating a cookbook is a labour of love that would not have been possible without the support, encouragement, and inspiration of so many incredible people. With my heart overflowing with joy, I express my gratitude to God for the inspiration to collate my culinary ideas and pictures and take people on this delightful journey with me.

A heartfelt thank you to my friends and extended family, who have not only shared meals with me but have also endured the unrelenting bombardment of pictures of my meals over the years. Your enthusiasm and feedback have been invaluable. My daughter Tolu, you surpassed yourself for the painstaking review of this book. I will do this with you all over again. Blessed by your creativity and eye for beauty - Loved Up

Pork Belly is a hit! Thank you.

"Write the vision, make it plain on tablets, so he may run who reads it..." - HAB 2:2. Feyishayo, my niece and indefatigable editor, you saw my vision and ran with it. So much energy! I cannot thank you enough. You made it easy. I would like to thank Stephanie for your instinctive kindness, the ad- hoc reviews and proofreading improved our editing. Abbie, without your help, I would be hawking the book out of a pannier on a bike! I couldn't be more grateful for your expertise and so much more.

My gratitude extends to the local supermarkets and farmers markets for providing the fresh, seasonal ingredients that have brought my recipes to life. Your commitment to quality produce has been instrumental in the success of this book. I remain thankful to Maple Publishers for your professionalism and patience throughout this process. We did it!

Finally, I want to thank each and every person who has ever dined at my table, tasted my food, and shared in the joy of a home-cooked meal. Your presence has given me the ultimate satisfaction of knowing that food can bring people together, create memories, and influence our choices for the better. This cookbook is a culmination of our collective experiences, and I am truly grateful for your role in its creation. 'We Do Easy' is not just a collection of recipes and ideas but a reflection of the love, support, and camaraderie that have nourished me on this culinary journey. From the bottom of my heart, I say thank you.